Rain Forest
Food Chains

Angela Royston

Chicago, Illinois

Edited by Claire Throp, Diyan Leake and Helen
Cox Cannons
Designed by Joanna Malivoire and Philippa
Jenkins
Original illustrations © Capstone Global
Library Ltd 2014
Picture research by Elizabeth Alexander and
Tracy Cummins
Production by Victoria Fitzgerald
Originated by Capstone Global Library Ltd
Printed and bound in China by Leo Paper Group

18 17 16 15 14
10 9 8 7 6 5 4 3 2 1

**Library of Congress Cataloging-in-
Publication Data**
Royston, Angela, 1945- author.
  Rain forest food chains / Angela Royston.
    pages cm.—(Food chains and webs)
  Includes bibliographical references and index.
  ISBN 978-1-4846-0518-9 (hb)—ISBN 978-1-
4846-0525-7 (pb) 1. Rain forest ecology—
Juvenile literature. 2. Food chains (Ecology)—
Juvenile literature. 3. Rain forests—Juvenile
literature. 4. Wildlife conservation—Juvenile
literature. I. Title.

QH541.5.R27
577.34—dc23   2013040532

Acknowledgments
We would like to thank the following for
permission to reproduce photographs: Alamy
pp. 11b (© Danita Delimont), 19 (© A & J Visage),
24, 25 chimpanzee (© National Geographic
Image Collection), 25 caterpillar (© Nick
Greaves), 27 (© imagebroker); Corbis pp. 10
(© Brian A. Vikander), 17 ant (© Mark Moffett/
Minden Pictures), 17 lizard (© Stephen Dalton/
Minden Pictures), 23a (© Natural Selection
David Ponton/Design Pics), 23c, 25 fruit (©
Konrad Wothe/Minden Pictures), 25 eagle (©
Natural Selection David Ponton/Design Pics),
25 millipede (© Gerry Ellis/Minden Pictures);
26 (© Tim Fitzharris/Minden Pictures), 29 (©
Scubazoo/SuperStock); Getty Images pp. 22
(Tim Makins), 25 monkey (Bruno Morandi),
28 (Mark Carwardine); Science Source p. 17
tree (Jacques Jangoux); Shutterstock pp. 1,
13 (© leungchopan), 4 (© Matt Tilghman), 5
(© Jim Leary), 7, 11c, 12 (© Dr. Morley Read),
8 (© javarman), 9, 14, 25 frog (© Aleksey
Stemmer), 11a (© Christian Vinces), 15 (©
worldswildlifewonders), 17 cobra (© Skynavin),
17 tree snake (© asyrafazizan), 16 (© Microstock
Man), 18 (© neelsky), 20 (© Ammit Jack), 21
(© apiguide), 23b, 25 duiker (© Four Oaks), 25
guava (© chai kian shin).

Cover photograph of red-eyed tree frog
reproduced with permission of Alamy
(© Martin Shields).

We would like to thank Michael Bright for his
invaluable help in the preparation of this book.

Every effort has been made to contact copyright
holders of material reproduced in this book.
Any omissions will be rectified in subsequent
printings if notice is given to the publisher.

All the Internet addresses (URLs) given in this
book were valid at the time of going to press.
However, due to the dynamic nature of the
Internet, some addresses may have changed,
or sites may have changed or ceased to
exist since publication. While the author and
publisher regret any inconvenience this may
cause readers, no responsibility for any such
changes can be accepted by either the author
or the publisher.

006968LEOF14

Contents

Some words are shown in bold, **like this.**
You can find out what they mean by
looking in the glossary.

What Is a Tropical Rain Forest?

Most rain forests grow in places that are hot and wet all year round. Tropical rain forests are full of life. Plants grow closely packed together, and many trees grow very tall.

Many types of plants grow in rain forests.

A toucan lives among the treetops.

Millions of animals live in the rain forest. Some live on the ground or in the **undergrowth**. Many others live in the treetops. What do they all eat?

Where Are Rain Forests?

Tropical rain forests grow in hot countries close to the Equator. The map shows where the world's largest rain forests are.

The largest rain forests are marked on the map in dark green.

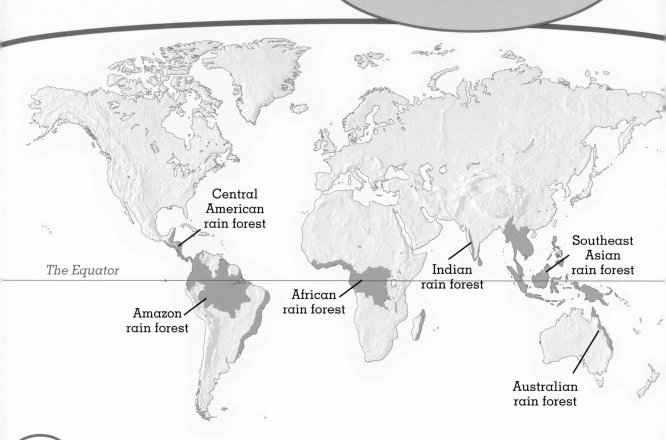

Central American rain forest

Southeast Asian rain forest

The Equator

Indian rain forest

Amazon rain forest

African rain forest

Australian rain forest

The Amazon River flows through the Amazon rain forest.

Rain forests used to be much larger, but people cut down the trees to sell the wood and to farm or mine the land. About half of the rain forests have been cut down.

Biggest rain forest

The Amazon rain forest is the world's largest rain forest. It covers an area about half the size of the United States.

What Is a Food Chain?

A **food chain** shows how food connects animals and plants in a particular **habitat**. The **energy** in food is passed from plants to each of the animals in the chain.

An orangutan uses its feet like hands to move through the trees.

A tree frog clings to a rain forest tree.

Living things need energy to grow and survive. For example, orangutans use energy to swing through the trees. Tree frogs use energy to breathe and to croak.

An Amazon Food Chain

The **food chain** on page 11 can be found in the Amazon rain forest. Tapirs eat shrubs and other leaves. **Energy** passes from the leaves to the tapir and then to the jaguar. As the tapir snuffles through the **undergrowth**, it does not see the jaguar hiding in the bushes. The jaguar pounces on the tapir and eats it.

Food chain

A jaguar feeds on the tapir

Tapirs eat twigs and leaves

Shrubs grow on the forest floor

Plants and the Sun

The jaguar eats the tapir, but the tapir eats plants. Without the plants, neither animal could survive. All **food chains** begin with plants, because only plants can make their own food.

Green plants make sugar in their leaves.

Bananas grow wild in many tropical rain forests.

Plants are called **producers**, because they use **energy** from sunlight to make sugary food. The sugar feeds every part of the plant, including the fruit.

Animal Diets

Animals are called **consumers**, because they consume food that they find in their environment. **Carnivores**, such as jaguars and poisonous frogs, hunt other animals. **Herbivores**, such as tapirs and deer, munch on plants.

This frog's blue skin warns other animals that it is poisonous.

A quetzal eats lots of different things.

Many animals eat both meat and plants. They are called **omnivores**. A quetzal, for example, eats mostly fruit, but it also catches lizards, frogs, and insects.

A Southeast Asian Food Chain

Most **food chains** have only three or four links, but some food chains are longer. The animals in this food chain all live in the treetops in Southeast Asia. **Energy** passes from the trees to the tree ants and on through the flying dragon and tree snake to the king cobra.

Rain forest in Southeast Asia

Food chain

A tree snake kills
and eats a lizard

A king cobra swallows
a tree snake

A flying dragon lizard
feeds on tree ants

Tree ants feed on
starch from the tree

A tree grows
in the forest

Top Predators

The animals at the end of a **food chain** are called top **predators** because they are not hunted by other animals. They include jaguars, tigers, and large snakes.

A tiger is a fierce hunter.

A reticulated python is a top predator.

Reticulated pythons are the longest snakes in the world. They coil themselves around **prey** and choke it to death. Then they slowly swallow their prey whole.

Scavengers and Decomposers

Scavengers, such as vultures, are animals that feed on the flesh of dead animals. Some insects lay their eggs in rotting flesh. The eggs hatch into maggots, which then feed on the flesh.

Vultures help to clear the forest of animal remains.

Forest fungi help to break up rotting tree trunks.

Decomposers include worms, insects, fungi, and bacteria. Decomposers break up the remains of plants and animals and turn them into soil.

A Congo Food Chain

The Congo rain forest is the second-largest rain forest in the world. In this **food chain, energy** passes from the fruit to the duiker and then to the eagle. The crowned eagle is a top **predator.**

The Congo rain forest

Food chain

An eagle swoops down and snatches the duiker

A blue duiker eats fruit and leaves

This fruit has fallen to the forest floor

Food Webs

Most animals belong to several **food chains.** Animals compete for food and may be food for several **predators.** The **food web** on page 25 is from the Congo rain forest. It shows how food chains link together to form a web.

Chimpanzees eat mainly fruit, but they occasionally eat red colobus monkeys, too.

Food web

crowned eagle

chimpanzee

blue duiker

red colobus monkey

tree frog

fallen leaves and fruit

caterpillar

giant millipede

guava

Important Links

Some animals or plants help the whole **habitat.** For example, in Borneo and Sumatra, orangutans wander around, eating fruit and dropping the seeds of many different plants.

A baby orangutan loves to eat fruit.

A cassowary spreads the seeds of large fruit in the Australian rain forest.

The seeds grow into plants that feed many different animals, and so the whole habitat is better off. In places with few orangutans, there are many fewer plants and animals.

Protecting Food Chains

People are the biggest threat to **food chains**, because they are cutting down the rain forest. For example, in Southeast Asia, the rain forests are being cleared so that palm oil can be grown instead.

Oil palms have been planted in place of rain forest trees and plants.

Big machines have cleared many areas of rain forest.

Unless people work together to preserve the rain forest, the orangutans and other rain forest animals will have nowhere left to live.

Glossary

carnivore animal that eats only the meat of other animals

consumer living thing, particularly an animal, that feeds on other living things, such as plants and other animals

decomposer living thing, such as an earthworm, fungus, or bacterium, that breaks up the remains of plants and animals and turns them into soil

energy power needed to do something, such as move, breathe, or swallow

food chain diagram that shows how energy passes from plants to different animals

food web diagram that shows how different plants and animals in a habitat are linked by what they eat

habitat place where something lives

herbivore animal that eats only plants

omnivore animal that eats plants and animals

predator animal that hunts other animals for food

prey animal hunted for food

producer living thing, such as a plant, that makes its own food

scavenger animal that feeds off the flesh and remains of dead animals

undergrowth plants in a forest that grow thickly together close to the ground

Find Out More

Books

Facthound offers a safe, fun way to find web sites related to this book. All the sites on Facthound have been researched by our staff.

Here's all you do:

Visit www.facthound.com

Type in this code: 9781484605189

Web sites

kids.nceas.ucsb.edu/biomes/rainforest.html
This web site has lots of information and fun facts about rain forests.

www.rainforest-alliance.org/kids
This web site is all about rain forests.

www.sheppardsoftware.com/content/animals/kidscorner/games/ foodchaingame.htm
Find out about food chains and test how much you know by playing the food chain game on this web site.

Index